COLOSSIANS

COLOSSIANS

A Study Guide for Women
by Juanita Stauffer

CALVARYgrace

2016

Colossians: A Study Guide for Women

Copyright © 2016 by Juanita Stauffer.

Published by Calvary Grace Church of Calgary
204 6A Street NE
Calgary, Alberta T2E 4A5
www.calvarygrace.ca

Cover design: Jamie Ballak

First Printing 2016

Trade paperback ISBN: 978-0-9949882-8-7
PDF ISBN: 978-0-9949882-9-4
Mobipocket ISBN: 978-1-988239-00-2
ePub ISBN: 978-1-988239-01-9

Contents

Foreword

Ever since the 16th century, when William Tyndale labored on his translation of the Bible, English speakers have read and studied the word of God in their own language. Tyndale's amazing work made the Scriptures accessible to the non-specialist. Tyndale's hope was for even "a boy that driveth the plough to know more of the Scripture." This goal could only be achieved by doing the work of transferring the meaning of Greek, Hebrew, and Aramaic words into English ones.

To have that work done for us is a great privilege, yet it is something that is easily undervalued. With so many English Bibles available today in numerous translations and formats, familiarity has bred contempt. The English Bible is so accessible that we often fail to work at knowing it at all. Yet we must work. We must study. We must complete the task that translation began by applying the truths of the Word of God to our own lives and contexts.

The purpose of this book, *Colossians: A Study Guide for Women,* is to offer assistance in the task of applying the Bible to daily life. As a guide to Bible study, it shares Tyndale's motive "to know more of the Scripture." As a guide for women in particular, it is designed to assist you as a Christian woman in your discipleship to Jesus Christ. By working through this study, you will gain insight into Paul's letter to the Christians at Colossae. As you do so, you will also gain insight into something even more critically important. This is, indeed, the very same thing that was the motive behind Tyndale's labor of translating the Scriptures—to know what it is to be "in Christ" through the Gospel.

As you work through Juanita Stauffer's book, you will encounter Paul's New Testament letter to the Colossians. Most likely, you will do this as a non-specialist. But you will also do it with the same spirit as

Tyndale, studying the Scriptures in order to know that "your life is hid with Christ in God" (Col. 3:3).

Clint Humfrey
Lead Pastor,
Calvary Grace Church of Calgary

Using This Study Guide

This study is set up for both personal study and group discussion. Some women are only able to attend a study with no time for homework whereas others have the time to do daily study. Therefore, this study is designed to meet varying levels of commitment. You may choose from three different levels of study:

1. Attend the group discussion time and participate without having done the homework.

2. Complete only the group discussion questions, found at the beginning of each week. Each set of questions covers the weekly passage.

3. Complete all the group discussion and individual study questions. There are four days of personal study, which go into more depth, in addition to the discussion questions. Together, they are probably best covered in five to six days of personal study. Those who have done the personal studies will also be able to contribute additional observations to the group discussion.

There are nine weeks of study, outlined below.

Week 1 – Outlining, Introduction, chaper 1, verses 1-2 – to be completed together in the first group discussion time. If you have time, read the book of Colossians one to four times before the first discussion time together.

Week 2 – Colossians 1:3-14

Week 3 – Colossians 1:15-23

Week 4 – Colossians 1:24 – 2:5

Week 5 – Colossians 2:6-10

Week 6 – Colossians 2:11-23

Week 7 – Colossians 3:1-15

Week 8 – Colossians 3:16-4:1

Week 9 – Colossians 4:2-18

Finally, this study was prepared using the English Standard Version (ESV) translation of Colossians. Accordingly, if you are using a different translation as you use this study, simply be aware that specific words or phrases discussed in this guide might differ slightly in the translation you are using.

Background Information

Paul wrote this letter to the believers in Colossae. The church was established in Colossae around AD 53-55 and Paul wrote from prison in Rome around AD 62. His imprisonment would have followed his journey recorded in Acts 27 and 28. The letter was likely sent with the letters to the Ephesians (Eph. 6:21) and to Philemon and was carried by Tychicus, a trusted disciple.

Ephaphras had come from Colossae to Rome and reported to Paul about a new problem in Colossae. Very little is known about the heresy Paul is addressing in Colossians. However, commentators generally believe it was Jewish in origin, and that it was an early and simple form of hyper-spirituality which despised the physical world and focused only on the spiritual, leading to asceticism and legalism. It included the worship of angels and saw them as mediators between God and man.

Week 1
Overview & Colossians 1:1-2

Overview

Read the letter to the Colossians aloud in your group to begin.

1. Who is the author of Colossians? Who is likely the physical writer of the book?

2. What do you learn about Paul in the book of Colossians? (See, for example: 1:1; 1:24; 4:2-4; 4:7-18. You can include other verses, too.)

3. Based on your readings of Colossians so far, what is the theme of the book?

4. Outline the book below (try not to use your Bible's titles):

1:1-2 _____

1:3-14 _____

1:15-23 _____

1:24-2:5 _____

2:6-10 _____

2:11-23 _____

3:1-15 _____

3:16-4:1 _____

4:2-18 _____

Group Discussion of Colossians 1:1-2

1. How is the greeting similar and different from other greetings in Paul's epistles? (See: Rom. 1:1-7; 1 Cor. 1:1-2; 2 Cor. 1:1-2; Gal. 1:1-2; Eph. 1:1-2; Phil. 1:1-2; 1 Thes. 1:1; 2 Thes. 1:1-2; 1 Tim. 1:1-2; 2 Tim. 1:1-2; Tit. 1:1-4; Philem. 1:1-3).

2. What is an apostle? Why is it important that Paul is "an apostle of Jesus Christ by the will of God"?

3. Paul calls Timothy his "brother" here. He also refers to Timothy as his son in the faith in First Timothy 1:2. What does the term "brother" reveal about Paul?

4. Read First Corinthians 1:1-2. How do these verses explain what a "saint" is?

5. How does Paul regard those to whom he is writing?

6. What does he hope for them in this greeting?

7. Where would you be if God had not given you grace and peace? How does this relate to the Gospel?

8. Read Colossians 4:18. How does Paul end the letter? Based on your first reading of the book, how does Paul give grace through this letter?

9. Discuss any questions you had in your readings of Colossians this week, but be prepared to put aside the questions until the end of the study.

COLOSSIANS: *A Study Guide for Women*

Weekly Prayer Requests or Further Notes

Week 2

Colossians 1:3-14

Group Discussion of Colossians 1:3-14

Begin by reading Colossians 1:3-14 aloud.

1. Paul offers both thanksgiving and prayer to God for the Colossians. How is he thankful?

2. What and when does he pray for them?

3. Remember that Paul has never met these Christians. He has only heard about them from Ephaphras. How does this encourage you to pray for Christians you have never met?

4. Read Ephesians 1:15-23. How does this passage add to our understanding of "the knowledge of his will"?

5. Ephesians 1:15-23 also helps us to understand how we might increase in our knowledge of God (Col. 1:10). What else do you learn in this passage that would help in this knowledge?

6. Colossians 1:10 speaks of walking in a manner "worthy of the Lord." What aspect of God's character would we consider in this instance? (See 1 Pet. 1:13-18).

7. Paul asks that the Colossians "be strengthened with all power, according to His glorious might." Read Ephesians 1:20 and Romans 6:4. How did God demonstrate his might according to these verses?

8. What does that tell us about God's ability to strengthen us?

9. What is the "inheritance of the saints in light"? (See Eph. 2:19 and Gal. 4:1-7).

10. Paul contrasts two kingdoms in verse 13. What are the two kingdoms? (Read Eph. 6:10-12).

11. What do we have in Christ? What is "redemption"? (See Eph. 1:7).

12. There are two areas of application in this passage. First, write down what Christians receive as a result of being transferred to God's kingdom.

13. Next, write down what right activities should result from God's grace being given to us.

14. Finally, write down how Paul prayed for the Colossians.

15. Consider your own life. How are you walking in the Lord this week?

16. Consider those you know. How can you learn to pray better for them?

17. In your group, pray for each other, that you might understand both the glorious riches of God's grace and how to respond to God's grace. And then use Paul's prayer to pray for others, both Christians and non-Christians, that they may truly understand both aspects of God's grace.

Week 2, Day 1

1. Read verses 3-14. What is the main idea of this passage?

2. In verse 3, Paul tells them that he does two things for them. What are they?

3. What is Paul's attitude toward the Colossians? How does he know about them?

4. What do we learn about Epaphras in verses 7-8? (Read also Col. 4:12 and Philem. 23).

5. From whom did you personally learn "the word of truth, the Gospel"? Notice the connection between Paul, Epaphras, and now the church in Colossae. Are there people in your life who need to hear the Gospel? Write their names down and pray for them today.

Week 2, Day 2

1. Why does Paul gives thanks to God for the Colossians?

2. What has Paul heard about the Colossians?

3. Notice the triad of faith, hope and love. This is a common theme in Paul's writings (read 1 Thes. 1:3; 5:8; 1 Cor. 13:13). What are the similarities and differences between the three passages?

4. Read Romans 5:1-8 and 8:23-24. How would you describe this hope?

5. This hope has both a present and a future aspect. Describe both.

6. What has come to the Colossians? How would you define it from this passage?

7. What is the fruit, and what is it a result of?

Week 2, Day 3

1. In verse 9, what is the reason Paul prays for the Colossians?

2. Paul asks God to fill them with what?

3. Where does the "spiritual understanding" come from? How are the members of the Trinity working together?

4. Read Romans 12:1-2. How do we receive the knowledge of God's will according to this passage?

5. Read verses 10-12. F.F. Bruce says, "Right knowledge… leads to right behavior." Write down some of the responses to God's work listed in this passage.

6. How can we "walk in a manner worthy of the Lord"? (Read Eph. 4:1-3; 5:1-7; 1 Thess. 4:1-8).

Week 2, Day 4

1. In verse 10, part of Paul's prayer is that the Colossians will be "bearing fruit in every good work." Why is it important to do this? (Read John 15:1-8).

2. What might that fruit look like? (See Gal. 5:22-23).

3. Where does the power to act rightly come from?

4. Why is it important to have "endurance and patience with joy"?

5. What should be the result of God's grace and power being extended to us?

6. What are we to thank God for?

Weekly Prayer Requests or Further Notes

Week 3
Colossians 1:15-23

Group Discussion of Colossians 1:15-23

Begin by reading Colossians 1:15-23 aloud.

1. Read Colossians 1:15-23. How are these verses a result of the prayer in verses 3-14?

2. What does "preeminent" (1:18) mean?

3. Read Colossians 1:15-23. How is Christ the Preeminent One in the verses that follow?

• Verses 15-17

• Verse 18

• Verses 19-20

• Verses 21-23

4. Why is it important that Christ is "the image of the invisible God"? (See Heb. 1:2-4; John 14:9).

5. How does Christ's incarnation help us to understand more about who God is?

6. How is Christ "the firstborn of all creation"? Note that "firstborn" relates to Christ's preeminence, not his origin. (See Jn. 3:16 and Gal. 3:26).

7. What is the extent of Christ's reign? (Consider also Rev. 3:14; Ps. 2).

8. Look up Romans 12:3-8 and Ephesians 4:4-6. How is Christ the head of the church, the body? Describe some of the work of the body.

9. If Christ is not the firstborn and is not preeminent, what difference would that make to our faith? (See 1 Cor. 15:12-19).

10. Verse 19 says that "all the fullness of God was pleased to dwell" in Christ. What does this mean? (See Heb. 1:1-4).

11. What is the means by which Christ reconciles all things to himself?

12. What was the relationship between God and man before Christ's death on the cross?

13. In verses 21-22, Paul contrasts two types of character and behavior. Compare the two and discuss what each type of character would be like, and what each type would do.

14. What does it mean to be "above reproach"? Read Ephesians 5:27 to read a description of the church Christ is presenting.

15. In Colossians 1:3-8, the Colossians are commended for their faith in Christ and the truth of the Gospel. What is their faith based on in verse 23?

16. How does Paul see his personal ministry in verse 23?

17. The Colossians had been believers for a few years at this time. Reflect on how their initial enthusiasm may have waned and how the admonition from Paul in verse 23 would help them to refocus.

18. How would this whole passage help the Colossian Christians to understand the truth of the Gospel and to stand firm against false teaching?

19. Given that Christ is preeminent, how does this help you to put your anxieties and worries into perspective?

20. As you pray together, thank God for each of the areas that Christ is preeminent, and pray for the Holy Spirit's help in your lives for each of these emphases.

Week 3, Day 1

1. Read Colossians 1:9-15. There are two persons referred to in the pronouns. Who are these two?

2. Who is the "He" in verse 15? What do we learn about him in verses 15-17?

3. What does it mean to be the "image of the invisible God"? (See 2 Cor. 4:4; Jn. 1:18). Consider how the nature and being of God is revealed in Christ.

4. Why is it significant that Christ is named the "firstborn"? (Consider Gal. 3:26; 1 Cor. 15:20-23).

5. How did all things come into being, according to verse 16? How would this help the Colossians to stand firm against the heresy of spiritual beings being mediators to God that was creeping into the church?

Week 3, Day 2

1. Consider John 1:1-4 and Hebrews 1:1-4. How do these passages further our understanding of verses 15-17?

2. According to verse 18, of what is Christ the head?

3. What does the head of a body do compared to what the body does? How does this apply to the church?

4. What difference does it make to the body of Christ that Christ rose from the dead and became the "firstborn from the dead"? How does he give life to the body?

5. Look up 1 Corinthians 12:12-27. Describe some of the functions of the body of Christ.

6. How does Christ being "preeminent" show God's power?

Week 3, Day 3

1. Read verses 19-20. How did the fullness of God dwell in Christ? (See Jn. 1:14).

2. What does God's pleasure in having his fullness dwell in Christ tell us about his nature?

3. What does it mean to be reconciled? What does this imply about the relationship between two people?

4. How does Christ reconciling all things to himself demonstrate his preeminence?

5. Why is it important that Christ made "peace by the blood of his cross"? (See 1 Pet. 3:18; Rom. 3:21-26).

Week 3, Day 4

1. Read verses 21-22. What is our relationship to Christ before salvation? (See Eph. 2:1-10).

2. In Paul's time, the relationship between Jews and Gentiles was hostile. How did Christ's sacrifice change this relationship? (See Eph. 2:14-18).

3. How can it change our relationships?

4. What is the reason for Christ's action of reconciliation, according to verse 22?

5. How important is it for Christians to continue in their faith? (See Phil. 2:11-12).

6. What is the foundation of our faith?

7. How are we able to remain firm in the faith?

Weekly Prayer Requests or Further Notes

Week 4

Colossians 1:24-2:5

Group Discussion of Colossians 1:24-2:5

Begin by reading Colossians 1:24-2:5 aloud.

1. Read Colossians 1:15-2:5 aloud. What is the connecting idea between 1:15-23 and 1:24-2:5?

2. Read Colossians 1:24-2:5. Summarize the main idea of this passage.

3. Break the passage into two parts: 1:24-29, and 2:1-5. What title would you give to each section?

4. What is Paul's view toward his sufferings? (See 2 Cor. 7:4).

5. Why is Paul willing to suffer in his ministry? (See also Eph. 3:13).

6. What is the reason that Paul carries on in this ministry? (Consider verses 23-25).

7. What is the mystery that has been hidden? For how long has it been hidden, and to whom has it been revealed? (Read verses 26-27, and consider also Eph. 3:1-13).

8. Why is it important that the mystery has been revealed to the Gentiles through Paul's ministry?

9. What phrase does Paul use to summarize the mystery?

10. In verse 28, Paul says that they preach Christ, warning and teaching everyone. How are warning and teaching different, and why would he include both?

11. Paul says he proclaims Christ "with all wisdom." Where does this wisdom come from? Why is it important that wisdom is part of the teaching and exhorting in a church? (See Prov. 1:7).

12. What is the reason that Paul preaches Christ to them?

13. Summarize Paul's attitude toward the Colossians and others in the area.

14. What hope does he have for them?

15. Epaphras has brought back some questions to Paul from the Colossians, which is why he writes this letter. What was the false teaching that was threatening the church? How seriously does Paul take the dangers of the false teaching they have been encountering?

16. Colossians 1:23 and 2:5 both describe how the Colossians' faith should be. Write down what Paul says about their faith.

17. How can your faith be shaken? What have you learned from these weeks of study that would help to strengthen your faith in times when it is wavering?

18. Pray for each other for faith in times of stress or unbelief. Pray for your church family and others who are struggling with the temptations of false teaching.

Week 4, Day 1

1. Read Colossians 1:15-2:5. What are the main ideas of this passage?

2. How does Paul view his ministry in verses 23-25?

3. Read Romans 15:15-21. How does Paul describe his ministry in this passage? What is similar or different from the way he describes it in Colossians?

4. How was Paul's ministry different from that of the other apostles? (Read Eph. 3:8 and Gal. 2:6-10).

5. What does it mean when Paul says, "I fill up in my flesh what is still lacking in regard to Christ's afflictions"?

"He was a suffering preacher: *Who now rejoice in my sufferings for you*, Col. 1:24. He suffered in the cause of Christ, and for the good of the church. He suffered for preaching the gospel to them. And, while he suffered in so good a cause, he could rejoice in his sufferings, *rejoice that he was counted worthy to suffer*, and esteem it an honour to him. *And fill up that which is behind of the afflictions of Christ in my flesh.* Not that the afflictions of Paul, or any other, were expiations for sin, as the sufferings of Christ were. There was nothing wanting in them, nothing which needed to *be filled up.* They were perfectly sufficient to answer the intention of them, the satisfaction of God's justice, in order to the salvation of his people. But the sufferings of Paul and other good ministers made them conformable to Christ; and they followed him in his suffering state: so they are said to fill up what was behind of the sufferings of Christ, as the wax fills up the vacuities of the seal, when it receives the impression of it. Or it may be meant not of Christ's sufferings, but of his suffering for Christ. He *filled that which was behind.* He had a certain rate and measure of suffering for Christ assigned him; and, as his sufferings were agreeable to that appointment, so he was still filling up more and more what was behind, or remained of them to his share."

Matthew Henry

6. Read verse 29. Compare it to Second Corinthians 1:3-8. Describe Paul's ministry.

7. How would you reconcile Paul's expression of "struggling and striving" with God's work in him? (Consider Matt. 11:28-30 as well). How does Paul continue on in his ministry, even when it is difficult?

8. Consider the ministry to which God has called you. This may or may not be an "official" ministry of the church. Consider your ministry to family and your job, as well as in the church. How is God calling you to suffer in this ministry?

9. What can you learn from Paul as you consider your ministry? In what ways do you need to learn to take all your burdens to Christ?

Week 4, Day 2

1. Read Colossians 1:25-27 and 2:2. What is the mystery Paul speaks of?

2. Read First Corinthians 2:6-13. How does this passage explain the mystery Paul speaks of in verses 26-27?

3. To whom has God's salvation been made known? (verse 27; read also Is. 49:6).

4. How is Christ "the hope of glory" (verse 27)? How does this encourage us today? (Read Rom. 11:33-36 and 2 Cor. 3:18).

5. Why is it important that Christ is proclaimed?

6. Where does the wisdom that Paul speaks of in verse 28 come from? Why is it important to our Christian walk?

7. "Wisdom" is a theme in Paul's letters. Read 1:28, and then go back to 1:9; look also at Ephesians 1:17-18. What do we learn about wisdom in these verses?

8. Pray Paul's prayer in Ephesians 1:15-23 and Colossians 1:9-10, asking God for wisdom and understanding this week.

Week 4, Day 3

1. Read Colossians 1:28-2:3. What is the reason that Paul preaches Christ?

2. What does it mean to be "mature in Christ"? (Some versions say "fully mature" [ex. NIV], or "perfect" [ex. NKJV]). Read also Ephesians 4:11-16.

3. What time frame is Paul referring to when he speaks of presenting men to Christ? (See 1 Thes. 2:19).

4. How does this encourage you?

Week 4, Day 4

1. Read Colossians 1:1–2:5 again. Note (or underline) all that Paul hopes for or wants the Colossians to know or be. Write them down below.

2. How does the Colossians' knowledge of Christ and who he is go with Paul's exertions on their behalf?

3. What does it mean to the Colossians that their "hearts may be encouraged, being knit together in love"? Give some examples of what this might look like in the church.

4. What is the goal of having their hearts united?

5. What does Colossians 2:2-3 teach us about the importance of the church?

6. Read First Corinthians 5:3-5. How does this passage, together with Colossians 2:5, show Paul's care and concern for other Christians who he is not with?

7. When we consider fellow members in our church or in other churches, what should we learn from Paul about our attitude towards them?

8. Pray for your church—for fellow members and the leadership of the church. Pray specifically that they would not succumb to false doctrine and that they would have a full understanding of the mystery of God, that is, Christ.

Weekly Prayer Requests or Further Notes

Week 5

Colossians 2:6-10

Group Discussion of Colossians 2:6-10

1. Read Colossians 2:6-10 aloud. What is the main idea of this passage?

2. In Paul's letters, he usually begins with the *"indicative."* He tells the reader what he or she needs to know about God. Make notes of what we have learned about God and Christ through the indicatives in chapters 1 and 2.

3. "*Imperatives*," what we should do, follow "*indicatives*," what we must believe. What two commands does Paul give in this passage?

4. The word used for "received" gives the idea of passing on a tradition and of handing it down from the apostolic authority to teachers to disciples. Jewish Christians were very familiar with this idea as it was the process by which the Old Testament was received. In 2:6, who has become the "tradition"? Where does the apostles' authority come from?

5. Two analogies are used in verse 7 to demonstrate the Colossians' faith. What are they?

6. Verses 6 and 7 and verses 8-10 contrast faith and doubt. Where do you see faith and doubt (unbelief) in these verses?

7. If Christ is the center of our faith, is faith active or passive? Where does it come from?

8. What should be our response to this faith and relationship?

9. What is the second command that Paul gives?

10. How could someone be taken captive by philosophy or deceit? What does that indicate about their understanding of Scripture?

11. The tradition received from the apostles is Christ. How is this contrasted in verse 8?

12. The theological term for Christ being both God and man is "*incarnation.*" How would this verse help to explain what incarnation is? (Consider also Jn. 1:14).

13. How does considering the incarnation help our unbelief?

14. Read Second Peter 1:4. Is being "partakers of the divine nature" and being "filled in [Christ]" (Col. 2:10) the same thing?

15. What does this tell us about our relationship with God and how we should live?

16. According to verse 10, Christ is the head of what? What does this comprise of?

17. How does this relate back to what we learned about Christ in Colossians 1:15-23?

18. Where in this passage do we find justification (being declared righteous) and sanctification (being made holy)?

19. Given that Christ himself is the foundation, what does it mean to "walk in him" (2:6)? (See Eph 2:10; 4:1; 2 Thes. 3:6). Give specific examples from your life of ways to apply this.

20. What worldly and deceitful philosophy threatens you at this time? What Scriptures and biblical ideas can you use to make sure that this doesn't take you captive?

21. How are you tempted towards unbelief? How does this passage you encourage you to fight against that unbelief?

22. As a group, write down all the ways you are thankful to God for His work in your lives. Use this list as a springboard for your prayer time tonight.

Week 5, Day 1

1. Read Colossians 2:1-10. Paul ended the first paragraph by exhorting them to not be deluded by "plausible arguments" (2:4) and reminded them of his joy in their faith. How does that prepare the reader for verses 6-10?

2. How is verse 6 a response to verses 1-5?

3. Write a brief paragraph describing how you "received Christ Jesus the Lord" (2:6). What did that look like in your life?

4. Read Romans 6:4, Ephesians 5:2, Colossians 1:10, and First John 2:6. How do these verses help explain the command to "walk in him" (Col. 2:6)?

5. How can you specifically apply this command to your life circumstances? What are ways that you struggle to apply this?

Week 5, Day 2

1. Read Psalm 1. The psalmist describes the person who is like "a tree planted by streams of water" (Ps. 1:3). Write down the description of this person, including the habits of her life.

2. How can these habits help you to be "rooted and built up in him and established in the faith" (Col. 2:7)?

3. What habits do you need to change or implement in your life?

4. According to Colossians 2:6, what flows out of the person who is rooted in Christ? To whom is this addressed?

5. Listen to your words today. Does what you say and do reflect someone who is "abounding in thanksgiving"?

6. Write down as many items as you can think of that you could be thankful for. Keep adding to the list this week. Pray that God will help you to be someone who is thankful and who expresses this thankfulness to God regularly.

Week 5, Day 3

1. Several times so far in Colossians, Paul has warned them about being deceived or moving away from their faith. Read chapter 1 verses 23 and 28, and chapter 2 verses 4 and 8. Why do you think it is easy for Christians to be deceived and drawn away?

2. What images come to mind when you read "takes you captive" (Col. 2:8)? What is the opposite of captivity?

3. Is all human philosophy wrong? How do you know which ones are acceptable? Consider *belief* and *unbelief* in your answer.

4. What was wrong about the "plausible arguments" (2:4) and "philosophy and empty deceit" (2:8) that Paul was warning the Colossians about?

Week 5, Day 4

1. Read Colossians 2:9. Describe in your own words what this verse is saying about Christ.

2. Read John 1:1-18, John 8:48-59, First Timothy 2:5, and Hebrews 1:1-4. Jot down how each helps to explain verse 9.

3. Note the tense in verse 10 ("and you have been filled in him"). Now read First Corinthians 6:9-11. What tense is used in verse 11?

Why is it important to notice that the past tense is used in both of these passages?

4. How does being "filled in him" relate to our justification in Christ?

Week 5: *Colossians 2:6-10*

Weekly Prayer Requests or Further Notes

Week 6
Colossians 2:11-23

Group Discussion of Colossians 2:11-23

1. Read Colossians 2:1-23 aloud. Several times in this chapter, the phrase "in him" or "with him" is used. To whom does it refer? List all the ways we are described to be "in/with him."

2. Recall the difference between *"imperative"* and *"indicative."* Read Colossians 2:11-16 again. Would you say this is more imperative or indicative?

3. What is circumcision, and how was it a part of the Old Testament religious system? (Read Gen. 17:9-14).

4. What does circumcision represent and how did it change in the New Testament? (See Deut. 10:16; 30:6; Jer. 4:4; Rom. 2:28-29; Phil. 3:3).

5. Given the references in question 4, describe what a "circumcision made without hands" (2:11) is or looks like.

6. According to verses 11-12, how is the body of flesh "put off"? (Read Rom. 6:1-11).

7. How does sharing in Christ's death and burial help to circumcise our hearts and put off the sinful self?

8. What is the connection between faith, resurrection, and God's work in us?

9. According to Paul in verses 13-14, what were the Colossians like before their salvation? How have they been changed?

10. Consider verses 11-15 again. In your life, how is this a consolation and encouragement that God has done these things on your behalf? If you have not been baptized, consider the importance of this step.

11. Notice how Paul's commands flow from the "indicative" to the "imperative"? Why is this important and what difference does it make to our understanding of God's requirements of us and our responsibilities to Him?

12. In verses 16-23, Paul gives one command, but says it several different ways. How would you summarize the one command?

13. Who should we "hold fast to" instead? What is the result of holding fast?

14. How are you tempted to hold fast to regulations and not to Christ? What are some modern-day equivalents?

15. In Philippians 2:11-12, Paul commands believers: "...work out your own salvation with fear and trembling." How can we keep a balance between doing that and judging others in the areas we have talked about?

16. If you are feeling unsure about your salvation and confused by various voices apart from God's word, how does this passage encourage you? What truth does it speak and what do you need to remember this week?

17. Pray for each other in the areas of temptation you have talked about.

Week 6, Day 1

1. Read Colossians 2. Describe the main points of Paul's argument in this chapter.

2. How do verses 11-15 help to give the Christian freedom from "philosophy and empty deceit" (verse 8)?

3. Verse 11 says that they "were circumcised with a circumcision made without hands." What does this describe and how is it possible? (Refer to verses 12-15 to help you answer).

4. If the Colossians were feeling unsure of their salvation and confused by the heretical teachers, how could verses 13-15 reassure them?

5. Why is it important that Christ was raised from the dead, according to verse 12?

6. Pray through verses 11-12, thanking God specifically for what he has done in your life.

Week 6, Day 2

1. Read Colossians 2:13-15. What does it mean to be "dead in your trespasses and the uncircumcision of your flesh"? (Refer to Eph. 2:1-9 as well).

2. Read Ezekiel 37:1-14. How does this relate to what Paul tells us in this passage?

3. How did God cancel the "record of debt" (2:14)?

4. How is it significant that he nailed it to the cross? (See Eph. 2:15-16).

5. How long does this cancellation of our "record of debt" last for?

6. When you are tempted by guilt in remembering past sins, how will this passage help you?

Week 6, Day 3

1. Read Colossians 2:11-15. In verse 15, Paul may have had in mind the picture of a victorious Roman general parading his conquests behind his chariot in a victory parade. To whom is Paul referring when he speaks of "the rulers and authorities"? Through what means did Christ put them to shame?

2. Read verses 16-23. When Paul uses "therefore" at the beginning of this passage, what is he referring back to? Why should the Colossians not let anyone judge them in their practices?

3. The imagery of "shadow" in contrast to substance is used elsewhere. Read Hebrews 8:3-6 and 10:1-4. What is the shadow and what is the substance?

4. How does this help us to understand how to fight against the heresy that Paul is warning the Colossians about? What danger were the Colossians facing?

6. What dangers might we face in this area? What are the equivalent concerns of "questions of food and drink, or with regard to a festival or a new moon or a Sabbath" (2:16)?

7. What are we called to remember? What will happen as a result of clinging to the "substance of Christ"?

Week 6, Day 4

1. Read Colossians 2:20-23. If, as Paul says, we have "died to the elemental spirits of the world," why is it important that we don't submit to regulations?

2. Does this mean that we have complete liberty in everything we do, including sinning? Why not?

3. Why do regulations have no value in stopping the indulgence of the flesh? How can regulations actually keep us from God? Give an illustration of how that works in your life.

4. What is the alternative to living according to regulations? (See also Jn. 15 and Gal. 5:22-23).

Weekly Prayer Requests or Further Notes

Week 7

Colossians 3:1-15

Group Discussion of Colossians 3:1-15

1. Briefly recap Colossians 2:11-23. According to Paul, what is the Christian's status after salvation?

2. Read Colossians 3:1-15. Summarize the main idea of the passage without using the chapter headings from your Bible.

3. In verse 1, Paul uses an "if-then" statement. Compare and contrast this with the "if-then" statement in Colossians 2:20.

4. Chapter 3 is often referred to as the "put-off, put-on" chapter. What are we to put off and what are we to put on?

5. How do verses 3-4 help us to do this?

6. Another common command that arises from this chapter is "be what you are." Explain how the Scripture supports that statement.

7. How do we move from what we were to what we are? (See Rom. 6:11 and 8:13).

8. Some people might say that this chapter promotes legalism – believing that salvation is gained through good works, not faith. How would you argue against that using Colossians 3?

9. In verse 5, we have a list of sins. Notice how they move from an outward expression to an inner expression. How is covetousness idolatry and how does it contribute to the other sins in the list?

10. A second list of sins is in verses 8-9. Why does Paul adjure the Colossians to put away all these sins?

11. How does verse 10 help us with those sins?

COLOSSIANS: *A Study Guide for Women*

12. Paul has been talking about transformation—putting off old habits and sins. How does verse 11 relate to this "putting off"?

13. Verses 12-15 now move to the "putting on." Why should we "put on" these new habits?

14. Define each of the following terms and write an example of how you could exemplify this trait in your life:

Definition	Your application
Compassionate heart	
Kindness	
Humility	

Week 7: *Colossians 3:1-15*

Definition	Your application
Meekness	
Patience	
Bearing with one another	
Forgiveness	
Love	
Peace of Christ	
Thankfulness	

15. Go back and look at the sins in verses 5-9. How could the "putting on" habits help you fight the "putting off" habits?

16. Pick one or two applications from the chart to ask the group to pray for you. In your group prayer time, pray specifically for each other to apply what you have learned tonight.

Week 7, Day 1

1. Read Colossians 3:1-4. What is the "if-then" referring back to?

2. Why is it important to "seek the things that are above" (verse 1)?

3. According to Ephesians 1:20-22, describe what it means when it says, of Christ, that God "seated him at his right hand."

4. Ephesians 1:19 also says that God worked "his great might" when he raised Christ from the dead. Look back at Colossians 2:11-15. Why does Paul emphasize in Colossians 3:3 that "you have died" and how does that relate back to Ephesians 1:20 and Colossians 2:11-15?

5. According to verses 3 and 4, how are our lives different after salvation?

6. What changes in how we think and live are a result of our lives being "hidden with Christ in God"? (Read Matt. 6:19-21; Jn. 14:6; Rom. 6:2; 2 Cor. 5:7; and 1 Jn. 3:2-3).

Week 7, Day 2

1. What is the hope that Paul sets out in verse 4? Read First Corinthians 15:50-58 and write down how this passage expands on Colossians 3:5.

2. Read Colossians 3:5-9. Why are the Colossians being told to "put to death therefore what is earthly in you"? (Pay particular attention to the "therefore").

3. Jot down the lists of vices in the following passages.

• Romans 1:29-31

• 1 Corinthians 5:11

• 1 Corinthians 6:9-11

• Galatians 5:19-21

• Ephesians 5:3-6

• Colossians 3:5-9

What is the result of living according to the earthly nature (verse 6)?

4. Paul gives the list of sins, but then says: "In these you too once walked, when you were living in them" (3:7). Why, if he speaks of them in the past tense, does he still tell the Colossians to "put them all away" (verse 8)? (See Rom. 6 for more help with this).

Week 7, Day 3

1. Read verses 9-11. Why are we not to lie to each other?

2. Why do you think Paul ended his list with this command?

3. How can the new self be renewed in knowledge? (See Rom. 12:1-2; Eph 1:15-21; 3:14-19).

4. According to verse 11, what is the kingdom of God like? Why is this important?

5. How does having unity in Christ encourage you? (Read Gal. 3:27-28 as well).

Week 7, Day 4

1. Read Colossians 3:12-15. How does God view his people?

2. As a result of being holy and beloved by God, how are we to behave?

3. How do each of these traits relate to the others? If we miss any of them, what could happen?

4. Read Matthew 6:9-15. What is the result of unforgiveness? Why is forgiveness so important?

5. Verse 14 gives the one character trait that is over all the others. What is it? What does it do? Give an example of how this trait has made a difference in the relationships you have with others. Be specific.

6. How does having "the peace of Christ rule in your hearts" (3:15) make a difference to relationships with those around you?

7. Why do you think Paul concludes this section with "be thankful"?

Weekly Prayer Requests or Further Notes

Week 8

Colossians 3:16-4:1

Group Discussion of Colossians 3:16-4:1

1. Read Colossians 3:16-4:1. Paul ends Colossians 3:15 this way: "And be thankful." How does a theme of thankfulness continue on through these next verses?

2. What is "the word of Christ"? Do you think the admonition to "let the word of Christ dwell in you richly" is more for individual Christians or for the community of believers? Why or why not? What would be some of the ramifications of either view?

3. How can the word of Christ dwell "richly"? Discuss what this might look like in your church or life.

4. How should we be teaching and admonishing each other? Where does wisdom come from?

5. It's tempting to look at "psalms and hymns and spiritual songs" as three separate parts and styles. Instead, consider them as a whole. What is the purpose of singing to each other?

6. What is the purpose of our worship together? Reflect on how considering worship as mutual edification might change your view and practice in the church.

7. Look back over Colossians 1-3 and jot down some reasons you can sing "with thankfulness in your hearts to God" (3:17). How might being thankful go with the passage we studied last week with the "put ons"?

8. Consider verse 17 as a summary statement of verses 1-16. How does verse 17 affect the specifics given in the previous verses?

9. Is verse 17 more of a general principle or a specific command? Consider the following questions to be applied to specific situations. How could these questions help a Christian to make wise decisions without having specific instructions from the Bible for a situation?

> What is the Christian thing to do?
> Can I do this without compromising Christian confession?
> Can I do it "in the name of Jesus"?
> Can I thank God the Father through Him that He has given me the opportunity of doing this thing?
>
> E.K. Simpson and F.F. Bruce, *The Epistles of Paul to the Ephesians and to the Colossians*, The New London Commentary on the New Testament (1957), p. 286

The next few verses consider relationships within the Christian home and between an employer and employee, one or both of whom are believers.

10. How are wives to behave towards their husbands? What is the reason for this? (See also Eph. 5:22-33).

11. How are husbands to behave towards their wives?

12. What is the responsibility of children? What is the rationale behind this command?

13. "Fathers" in verse 21 can also refer generally to "parents." What is the responsibility of parents toward their children? What would be the result of being harsh with children?

14. According to verses 22-25, how are slaves to behave towards their masters? Why should they behave in this way?

15. According to Colossians 4:1, how are masters to behave toward their slaves?

16. Putting this into a modern context, summarize how employees and employers should relate to each other. What difference does it make if either or both are believers?

17. How can you apply this to your own situation? How does this apply to the "job" you have, whether it is paid or unpaid?

18. Review the "vices and virtues" from the first part of Colossians 3. In considering your specific role(s), what do you need to "put off" and what should you be "putting on"?

19. Pray for each other, applying these admonitions as you pray: Let God's word dwell in you; be thankful; do all for the glory of God; and be wise in the roles you inhabit. Take a few minutes to mention any prayer requests you have related to these admonitions and then spend time together in prayer.

Week 8, Day 1

1. Read Colossians 3:1-17. How do verses 16-17 sum up this passage?

2. How would you define "the message of Christ"? What are we to do with it?

3. Read Psalm 1, Psalm 119:9-16, and Philippians 4:8-9. How do these verses help us to understand the command to "let the word of Christ dwell in you richly"?

4. In what ways do you need to grow in your understanding and practice in this area?

5. How can we encourage each other in this? Do we need to be leaders in the church to apply verse 16? Who is it addressed to?

6. Write down three specific ways you could apply this during the next week.

Week 8, Day 2

1. Read Colossians 3:16-17 and James 3:13-18. Where does wisdom come from? What does it produce?

2. Read Ephesians 5:18-20. What is the result of being filled with the Spirit?

3. According to Colossians 3:16 and Ephesians 5:19, what is the purpose of worshipping God through song?

4. Reflect on the corporate worship at your church. How can you encourage others through your participation in the worship service? How can we serve others through the use of songs?

5. Paul sums up the passage in verse 17. How are we to live?

6. Consider all of verses 1-17. Why is thankfulness so important?

Week 8, Day 3

1. Paul moves from the general role of a Christian to specific roles of individuals. What general principles from verses 16-17 should be carried over to specific roles?

2. Read the parallel passage in Ephesians 5:22-6:9. Summarize the role of each person from each passage.

	Ephesians 5:22-6:9	Colossians 3:18-4:1
Wives		
Husbands		

	Ephesians 5:22-6:9	Colossians 3:18-4:1
Children		
Parents		
Slaves		
Masters		

3. Which of these roles apply to you? Consider the summary of each passage carefully. What insights have you gained as you've considered the commands here?

Week 8, Day 4

1. In verse 18, how does the phrase "as is fitting in the Lord" give dignity to the command for wives to submit to their husbands? (Consider also Gal. 3:27-28 and 1 Pet. 3:4).

2. In verse 19, what is the connection between husbands loving their wives and not being harsh with them? (Consider also 1 Pet. 3:7).

3. What is the expectation of children and what is the reason they should behave in this way? What are some ways parents can teach their children not only to obey but also the reason behind obedience?

4. How can parents avoid provoking children to anger while still expecting obedience? Why is it important for children to not become discouraged?

5. Think about the modern-day equivalent of slaves and masters being employees and employers. Although we may or may not work for pay, each of us will encounter situations where we are subordinate to someone else and where we are in leadership. List the ways slaves and masters were to behave and write a modern application for your life beside it.

Commands to slaves	Modern application

Commands to masters	Modern application

Weekly Prayer Requests or Further Notes

Week 9

Colossians 4:2-18

Group Discussion of Colossians 4:2-18

1. Read Colossians 4:2-18. How does this passage fit into the structure of the book as a whole?

2. Chapter 3 begins with an admonition to "set your minds on things that are above" (verse 2). What are two other ways believers can "set their minds on things above" according to 4:2-6?

3. Read Matthew 26:41 and Mark 14:38. What was Jesus' command to the disciples? Why is it important to be watchful in prayer?

4. Ephesians 6:18 is a parallel verse to Colossians 4:2. How does this verse add to your understanding of what Paul commands here?

5. In both Ephesians 6:19-20 and Colossians 4:3-4, Paul follows a command to pray with a specific prayer request for himself. What similarities and differences can you see between the two requests?

6. Who should you be praying for "that God may open ... a door for the word"?

7. Read 1 Peter 2:11-12. How do these verses add to your understanding of how we can be wise in the way we relate to unbelievers?

8. What does it mean to be "making the best use of the time" (4:5)? The NIV translation reads "make the most of every opportunity." Give some examples of ways you might be able to do that.

9. What is conversation that is filled with grace? Consider the positives and negatives in the following passages (this is just a small sampling of passages addressed to the tongue).

• Proverbs 16:23-24

• Ephesians 4:1-4

• Ephesians 4:25-32

• Ephesians 5:3-4

• James 3:1-12

10. How can gracious conversation lead to a good witness with outsiders?

11. How is the wisdom of verse 5 connected to knowing how to answer each person in verse 6? Where does this wisdom come from? (See also Prov. 1:7).

12. Read Colossians 4:7-18. What is your first impression regarding the people that Paul lists here? How can we be encouraged when we read a list like this?

13. We read about Epaphras already in Colossians 1:7-8. How is he described in chapter 1 and 4? What is his main work on their behalf?

14. If you have time, consider the questions in Day 3 of this study and discuss the people listed in more detail.

15. How does a list like this argue against a "lone-ranger Christian" mentality, where Christians say that they don't need the church? How does this encourage you to foster deeper relationships within the church?

16. In your prayer time, list and choose some of the following to pray for:

• the pastors and other leaders of your church

• people in whom God has been opening a door for your witness

• building relationships in your church family

• specific requests regarding making the use of every opportunity in witnessing

• gracious speech in all circumstances

Week 9, Day 1

1. In general, Paul used the first two chapters to set out the *"indicative"* (that is, what has God done for us?), and chapters 3-4 to set out the *"imperative"* (that is, how should we respond?). Take a few minutes to review and jot down the indicatives and imperatives of Colossians.

2. Read Colossians 4:2-5. Given that Paul is summing up the letter and providing final instructions, what is the background of the command to pray? Look at what you wrote down in question 1. How do these lead to the command to continue steadfastly in prayer?

3. Why is thankfulness important in prayer? How does it relate to the indicatives of the first two chapters?

4. What can you be thankful for today in your prayers? Be specific!

5. List all the aspects of "continuing steadfast in prayer." Consider both the time and effort involved.

6. What keeps you back from devoting yourself to prayer? Are you happy with your prayer life? What should you be asking God for as you consider it?

Week 9, Day 2

1. Read Colossians 4:2-5. Where was Paul at the time of this writing? Why did he want the Colossians to pray for him and what was he asking for?

2. Is there a situation in your life in which you desire God to open the door for the Gospel? Write it down and begin or continue praying that God will provide the opening for you.

3. When the door is opened to share the Gospel, what do we need to remember according to verses 5-6?

4. How can you be prepared to "make the most of every opportunity"?

5. Read First Peter 3:15. What else do you learn from this verse about being wise toward outsiders?

6. Read Matthew 5:13 and Ephesians 4:29. What is the purpose of salt? How can our conversation be "seasoned with salt"?

Week 9, Day 3

1. The following chart lists the people named in this chapter. Look up the other references to them and summarize what we know about them from the New Testament.

Tychicus	Col. 4:7-8; 2 Tim. 4:12; Tit. 3:12; Eph 6:21; Acts 20:4	
Onesimus	Philemon	
Aristarchus	Acts 19:29; 20:4; 27:2	
Mark	Col. 4:10; 2 Tim. 4:11; Acts 12:25; 15:36-41	
Justus	Col. 4:11	
Epaphras	Col. 1:7-8; 4:12-13; Philem. 23; Rom. 15:30	
Luke	Col. 4:14; 2 Tim. 4:11;	
Demas	Col. 4:14; 2 Tim. 4:10	

COLOSSIANS: *A Study Guide for Women*

Nympha	Rom. 16:5	
Archippus	Philem. 2	

2. What particular characteristics from this list stand out to you?

3. Paul says that he is sending Tychicus to them to "encourage [their] hearts" (4:8). Think about some ways you could encourage the hearts of those around you. How do you think this could affect your conversation with other believers?

Week 9, Day 4

1. Epaphras is described in 4:12 as someone who struggled or wrestled in prayer on the Colossians' behalf. What was the goal of his prayers?

2. What does God promise in James 5:16?

3. For whom are you wrestling in prayer this week? When you are tempted to give up because you don't see any answers, how does this promise encourage you?

4. What does it mean to "stand mature and fully assured in all the will of God" (4:12)? (See also Eph. 1:15-23).

5. Paul completes Colossians by writing "Grace be with you." Where does this grace come from? Remember this as you pray today.

Week 9: *Colossians 4:2-18*

Weekly Prayer Requests or Further Notes

About Calvary Grace Church

Calvary Grace Church is an evangelical partnership of believers in Jesus Christ committed to seeing God glorified in the area of Calgary, Alberta, Canada and beyond.

We are gathered around the expository preaching of God's Word and hold to the theology of the Protestant Reformation, striving to become more like Christ and to proclaim the Good News of his Kingdom in gratitude to the God who saved us by his sovereign grace.

For more information, please visit our website at:

www.calvarygrace.ca

CALVARYgrace

www.ingramcontent.com/pod-product-compliance
Lightning Source LLC
Chambersburg PA
CBHW032005040426
42448CB00006B/490